Deer Hunting Guide: Whitetail Tactics

Everything You Need to Know to Successfully Bag a Trophy Quality Whitetail Buck

Andrew Saari

ISBN-10: 1477507388
ISBN-13: 978-1477507384

DEDICATION

To my wife, Jackie.

CONTENTS

1 DEER HUNTING 101: AN INTRODUCTION

As dawn breaks over the misty hills, a smoky aroma settles over the forest and the wind scatters the crispy leaves of late autumn on the ground beneath your stand.

Your back is stiff from sitting in your stand for the past several hours, but it is tolerable, because you know that in just a few moments, the buck you have been scouting is going to present himself. You are both excited and completely calm at the same time.

A slight breeze blows gently in your face, but you're also warmed by the growing sunlight behind you. Your position is perfect: the deer is upwind of you, and the light will be in his eyes, making him less likely to smell or see you. You're confident that you've done everything right this time.

But, you're also starting to have doubt. Based on your scouting, the buck should have started to make his way to the watering hole by now. Maybe you did something to startle it, or somehow gave away your position. You start to wonder, perhaps if…

Suddenly, he steps out from between a stand of trees where he has been waiting. This deer is cautious, which is probably why it has lived long enough to grow such a magnificent 12-point rack on its head.

This deer is beautiful. He's big, strong and simply majestic. This may be the most amazing deer you have ever seen anywhere. He stands perfectly still. The only thing moving is the tip of his nose, which seeks out the scent of any predators that may be nearby. Satisfied, he takes one step forward, stops, and then takes another step.

You silently lift up your rifle and position the beautiful buck in the crosshairs of your scope. Almost as if sensing this, the deer looks directly at you. You hold your breath, waiting to see if he will suddenly leap into the bushes, but instead the deer decides he is in no danger and begins once again to walk toward his drinking spot.

You take aim at your target, just behind the deer's front shoulder blade, and put your finger on your rifle's trigger.

If there's a heaven on earth, this is it, you think as you gently exhale and squeeze the trigger.

I have been hunting deer for more than three decades now, and the experience is just as rewarding today as it was the very first time I went out into the woods with my father and uncles all those many years ago. During the years in between, I've shot my share of whitetail deer and while every hunt has the same basic parts – scouting, planning, waiting and finally the kill shot – every hunt has been a unique experience, as well.

After many, many years of deer hunting, I still get excited during the days leading up to the start of the hunting season, as I gather my equipment and plan my hunt. It never gets old for me, and I doubt it ever will.

In this guide, I will be sharing many of the techniques and secrets that have made me a successful whitetail deer hunter over the years. I'll discuss the best gear you will need, where to find it, and how to select the hunting rifle that is perfect for you. I'll review some of the other weapons you can use to make your deer hunting experience exciting and fascinating, including shotguns, pistols and even bows and arrows.

I'll also be reviewing basic gun safety and how to avoid getting lost in the woods. I'll even be talking about scent control, weather patterns, and cloaking techniques.

Finally, I'll be reviewing the social life of deer, and how you can use it to your advantage when hunting a trophy buck. By the time you finish reading this guide, you will have everything you need to bag your prize buck and more importantly, enjoy a lifetime of fun and exciting whitetail deer hunting.

So what are we waiting for?! Let's get started!

2 A BEGINNER'S GUIDE TO HUNTING WHITETAIL DEER

People hunt for all kinds of reasons. Some people enjoy the primal thrill of tracking an animal through the woods, patiently waiting for exactly the right moment, then taking the majestic buck down with a perfectly placed kill shot. Others hunt for the food the animal can provide, filling their freezers with venison and smoking the meat for the long winter ahead. Still, others hunt because they want to mount their trophy's head above their fireplace mantle, and recount their tale of how it got there to anybody who will sit still long enough to listen.

Regardless of your motivation, hunting is one of the most enjoyable and interesting experiences you can have.

It gets you out into the wild outdoors at the height of nature's spectacular beauty, and it pits your will against the raw, untamed mind of a fully mature whitetail deer.

People have been hunting deer on this continent even before they started living indoors. In some ways, deer hunting today is carrying on a tradition that is as old as the land itself. When you aim your rifle at the deer, you are following in the footsteps of generations of people who came before you. It is a tradition that resonates in our very being.

But, the moment you squeeze the trigger of your rifle and deliver the shot that takes down your trophy buck is only the final step in a long process of preparation that begins weeks, even months, before. So many things go into planning and executing a successful hunt. And, in some ways, preparing for the hunt is the best part.

There are many types of deer that can be hunted in North America. This guide will be about hunting whitetail deer.

Whitetail deer get their name from the distinctive white patch of fur on the underside of their tails. The deer use this "white flag" as a distress signal to warn other deer of predators as they run away from danger. The rest of their coat is reddish-brown in the spring and summer, but it turns to more of a grey-brown as fall turns to winter.

The males are known as "bucks" and generally interact with females during the mating season, which occurs late in the fall. During the rest of the year, mature bucks tend to wander around either by themselves or in small groups of three or four. During the mating season, these groups tend to break up for the "rut" or the competition between males for the privilege of mating with the females.

Female deer are known as "does". They raise the young deer, called "fawns", and generally travel in family groups. Female deer without offspring usually travel alone.

For most of the year, whitetail deer spend all their time within about a single square mile. As herbivores, their days are centered around eating buds and small leaves, and finding an adequate water supply. But all that changes, at least for the bucks, during the rut when male deer have been known to travel many miles in a single day in search of a mate.

In a lot of ways, deer are like most people. They don't like a lot of change, and they tend to do the same things over again, day after day. They prefer to feed in an area where there are natural breaks in the terrain, such as between dense forest and a field. They like to use the forest for cover and the field to graze.

When deer bed down, they prefer areas where there is dense cover, but they also need adequate food supply and close access to water. This is one of the most important things for a hunter to know, because finding the bed of a buck is an important step toward bagging him.

Deer Seasons: A Practical Lesson

Deer have a predictable annual cycle. In the springtime, deer feed a lot to replenish the mass they have lost during the winter months. They enjoy grazing on the newly sprouted grass and low-hanging buds on trees and shrubs.

In the summer months, deer tend to eat more, because there is a nearly unlimited food supply. Deer can become bolder, venturing into areas you won't typically see them during the rest of the year, in order to find the richest, most nutritious food sources.

Mating season begins in the fall of the year, which is also when the vast majority of the deer hunting seasons are held. During this time of year, deer can be at their craziest as the bucks battle each other for the right to mate with the does. As the amount of sunlight per day shortens, their hormones go through the roof and the result can be a battle royale as male deer compete for dominance, often charging each other with their antlers.

Female deer are not immune to the craziness of the mating season. In order to attract mates, they will emit a musk that lets the males know they are ready to engage in intercourse.

Fall is also the time when deer gorge themselves on food, so they can store enough fuel to make it through the long, sparse winter months. In winter, there obviously is a smaller food supply, so deer have to spend more time foraging for food.

Many does are pregnant during the winter, giving birth to their fawns in the late winter and early spring, when the cycle starts all over again.

The dates for deer hunting season vary from state to state. There are even different seasons for hunting deer with different weapons. And in some cases, if there is an excessive amount of deer, some states will extend the season or declare special hunting seasons.

Many states require hunters to have a hunting license, as well as purchasing deer “tags”, which are licenses to shoot a single deer or a specified number of deer during a specifically defined deer season. This controls the number of deer that are hunted during a particular season, and allows state wildlife officials to control the size of the deer population.

Every state has slightly different deer hunting regulations. Even within the same state, there can be different regulations from county to county. To find out what the hunting rules are where you live, you can visit the website of your state's Department of Natural Resources, or pick up a copy of your area's regulations at your nearest hunting supplies store.

It's important that you understand and follow the rules where you hunt. Violating the rules is breaking the law, and can result in having your hunting equipment seized, being banned from getting a deer hunting license in the future, and even fines and imprisonment.

Most hunters tend to hunt in the state in which they live, because of the proximity to their homes. Also, out-of-state licenses tend to cost a lot more than resident licenses. But, if you live close to an area that has exceptional deer hunting – such as Wisconsin or Pennsylvania – it may be worth the extra money to get the out-of-state license.

Most hunters hunt bucks only. Does are less desired as a target. The does produce offspring, which are known as fawns. Shooting a doe not only removes the doe from the herd, but potentially one to two fawns per year out of the deer herd, as well. And, not to mention, the female fawns would also produce offspring in later years.

This has the potential to greatly reduce the number of deer in the herd in future years. If you need the meat to feed your family, go for it. They taste the same as bucks. But, if you're hunting for sport, let the doe go. Wait for a buck. You'll thank yourself in later years for the increase in your local deer population.

Respecting Nature: Balancing Sport with Spirit

Deer hunting is a fun and enjoyable sport, but it still involves taking the life of a marvelous and majestic creature. Hunters need to make certain that their harvesting is humane and respectful.

Native Americans would pray to the souls of the animals they kill as a way to honor their spirit. While it's not necessary for you to worship nature in order to respect it, you may find a kind of spirituality in the deep woods that non-hunters may never understand. When you take the life of your quarry, you can still respect all of the wonder of life, as well as nature itself.

Most hunters don't kill just for the sake of killing. Hunting is a way to appreciate nature's bounty, and have a respect for the natural order of the world. Hunting also helps control the deer population. Without hunters thinning the herd, deer would rapidly multiply to the point where there would be more deer than the food supply could support, and forests would become decimated. Disease and sickness could spread among the deer, and could potentially harm human populations, as well.

Hunting helps promote agriculture and the environment, and helps control the population of predators and animal pests.

Hunting gives us food we can use to feed ourselves and our families throughout the winter. What we can't use ourselves is often donated to charitable organizations to feed people less fortunate than ourselves.

Teaching our children to hunt educates them on self control, responsibility, compassion, humility and respect for the natural world. In fact, some studies have theorized that teaching boys to hunt decreases aggression, and helps them to become more peaceful, balanced men.

Then, there's the killing itself. For many non-hunters, this is the biggest hang up. The fact of the matter is that hunters strive to make the harvesting as humane as possible, with as little suffering as possible for the deer. A perfectly placed kill shot will kill a deer almost instantly. A careless or off-target shot can cripple an animal, or prolong its suffering. Good hunters will track wounded animals, and put them out of their misery as quickly as possible.

Finally, hunting supports conservation and wildlife management. Much of the money spent each year on hunting licenses and deer tags is used by state governments to maintain forests and keep natural areas free from pollution and development.

Ask any experienced hunter, and they will tell you: Hunting is one of the most respectful things we can do to honor nature and improve the world in which we live.

Five Critical Deer Hunting Lessons Every New Hunter Needs to Know

Before any new hunter goes off into the woods with a weapon, there are some critical rules he or she must know:

1. *The woods are a wild place and anything can happen* – Many hunters hunt deer in places where there aren't roads, or where there's little to no cell phone reception. Weather can change from a nice day in the woods to becoming dangerous quickly, and it's easy to become lost and disoriented. If you lack adequate food, water and shelter, it doesn't take long before you can be in real, life-threatening danger. Before you begin any hunting trip, always make sure somebody knows exactly where you are going and when you will return. That way, if you fail to return within

an established time frame, they can send a search party to find you.

2. *Weapons are dangerous and can kill you or somebody else* – Hunting rifles fire real bullets. Bows shoot sharp arrows. Hunting knives have sharp blades. They are not toys, and should be treated with respect. Aiming a loaded gun at anything other than your intended target is a very bad idea. When you are not using them, always make sure your weapons are not loaded and are securely locked in a place where children cannot get at them.

3. *There are other hunters in the woods, and they may not know you are not a deer* – Sometimes your camouflage can be too good, and another hunter may not be able to see you. Avoid getting injured or killed in a hunting accident by making other hunters aware of your presence, even if it means letting your buck know you're there, as well. It's not worth getting hurt over. When you master the techniques of hunting, there

will be plenty of other opportunities to bag a trophy buck. Wear brightly colored hunting clothes, so that other hunters can see you, or at the very least, make your presence known to them.

4. *The new deer hunting season starts the day after the old one ends* – While the actual hunting of deer is only legally allowed during a few short weeks, the planning and preparing for deer hunting is a year-round activity. Spending time in the woods observing the behavior of deer, looking for deer trails, and identifying the best places to set up your blind are some things the best hunters do all year round. Keeping your shooting skills sharp with target practice, selecting and preparing your equipment, and even practicing being silent for long periods of time are things hunters can do during the off-season to make their hunting time more valuable.

5. *There is a whole community of avid, enthusiastic hunters* – While many hunters prefer

to hunt solo, when you are not in the woods there are thousands of people in your area who share your passion for hunting whitetail deer. You can share your stories and tips with other hunters in online forums, at hunting clubs and events, and even at your local hunting supply store. Hunting is even more fun when you have somebody to talk to about it. Get the most out of your hunting experience by being a part of the hunting community in your area.

Why We Hunt: A First Person Account of What it All Means

Hunting is a great sport because it's fun, provides food, and it is something we can enjoy year round. But why do we enjoy hunting so much?

The answer lies in the act of hunting itself. It is a primal activity that addresses something deep in our own history. Man became the dominant species on earth, because he had the mental ability and the physical presence to hunt and kill other creatures.

When you aim your rifle and squeeze the trigger, you can be re-experiencing the same moment that all of your ancestors experienced, since the beginning of time. You may even feel a connectedness that resonates across the years all the way back to the first hunter, to the moment when man assumed his place at the top of the food chain.

Hunting also helps you to understand who you are. In many ways, you may define your life by some of the experiences you have had while hunting. You may even mark the months of your year by how close or far they are from hunting season.

After your first few hunting trips, you will begin to see how consuming and addictive it can be. But, unlike harmful addictions such as smoking or taking drugs, hunting is a positive addiction. It makes our lives richer, helps us to appreciate nature better, and it constantly teaches us lessons about who we are and why we are here.

3 HUNTING GEAR ESSENTIALS: WHAT YOU WILL NEED TO SUCCEED

One of the best things about hunting is that it can be enjoyed by anybody at any income level. If you are just starting out in life and don't have a lot of money yet, you can equip yourself with basic hunting gear for very little money. But, if you have been lucky enough in life to make a lot of money, you can spend as much as you want on your hobby, traveling to exotic places to hunt rare game, purchasing the latest technology and highest quality weapons, and indulging in your passion for hunting with endless abandon.

Most hunters fall somewhere in the middle of those two extremes. Hunting is not a super expensive hobby, and you don't have to be a highly trained athlete in order to excel at it. You just need to know what you're doing, and have the patience to wait for your shot. And, unlike other sports – such as golf, tennis or bowling – you get something for your money other than the entertainment the sport provides. You get a freezer full of deer meat!

The first step in determining what supplies you will need for your hunting trip is to figure out where you are going, and how long you plan to stay there. If you are going on a one-day hunting trip, you won't need a sleeping bag or tent. But, if you are planning on spending a week in the woods, your shopping list is going to be a lot longer.

Most hunting seasons are scheduled during cool or even cold weather, so dressing appropriately is important. Wearing layers of clothing provides the most warmth, and you can take off layers if you get too warm. You probably will want to have a waterproof outer barrier. Boots will protect your feet from dampness and sharp twigs and sticks, and wool socks will help keep your feet warm even during the coldest weather.

Wearing a hat is the best way to keep warm, because we lose as much as 90 percent of our body heat through the top of our heads. Gloves are important to keep our hands warm and dry, so we will be able to make the shot when the time comes. There are special hunting gloves you can buy that have a hole for your shooting finger to fit through, or you could just modify your existing gloves with a scissors or knife.

The most important thing to remember when you are in the woods is that you want to stay as warm and dry as possible. If you are stalking a buck, you aren't going to be able to build a fire. Drinking alcohol may make you feel warmer, but it will dull your senses and make you less able to bag a deer. Plus, it gives a false impression of comfort while your extremities are still exposed to the dangerous cold. Despite what you may have heard, drinking and hunting don't mix! Wait until you are back home or at the lodge before opening your first beer.

Rifles and other weapons will be discussed in the next section, so I won't spend a lot of time on them here. Suffice it to say that keeping your rifle dry is just as important – if not more important – than keeping yourself out of the rain and snow. A wet rifle can easily rust. That can not only result in your rifle not working properly, but could also be dangerous to you, as well.

Basic Hunting Equipment: Navigating the Sporting Goods Store

One of the most fun parts of getting ready for hunting season can be visiting the sporting goods store. That's because the hunting aisles are filled with cool gadgets and equipment that will make your trip more enjoyable. But, they can quickly drain your bank account, if you are not careful. Even though going to the sporting goods store is like visiting a toy shop when you were a kid, as an adult you need to be responsible enough so that you don't bankrupt your family and make your wife ask you for a divorce.

The best tip is to make a list of everything you need, before you go to the sporting goods store. Then, stick to that list once you get there. It’s easy to be tempted by all the goodies they have there, but once you start throwing extras into your cart, it’s hard to stop, just like when you go grocery shopping on an empty stomach.

While preparing your list prior to setting out, take the time to walk yourself through every step of your hunt - from the moment you park your car or truck, to the time you start your drive home. Where are you going? What will you do when you get there? How are you going to track your buck? If you have done your research, you already should have a pretty good idea of where you are going to place your stand. You should also know what kind of weather to expect when you get to your stand, or at least what you could potentially be in for.

Now that you have walked through your experience, take a look at the inventory of supplies you already have. You probably don’t need to replace everything each year. What supplies from last year can you still use again? What needs to be replaced? What new items are you planning to splurge on this year? Believe me, if you’ve been reading the hunting magazines and watching the hunting shows for the past year, you will probably have a pretty long wish list.

This list can include everything from the basics, like a compass, hunting coat, rifle, ammunition, targets for sighting in your rifle, a knife, boots, gloves and a hat, to the more advanced items like GPS units, game cameras, doe in heat scent, drip bags, wicks for your scents and even a new deer stand. The cost of all these goodies can add up in a big hurry.

You'll probably want to set a budget for yourself. Hunting is your entertainment, so it's not unreasonable to spend a little money on your hobby (at least that's what I keep telling my wife), but most people can't afford to go overboard either. Once you have a budget, take that amount in cash with you to the sporting goods store, and leave your credit cards at home. That way you won't be tempted to buy all those cool extras you see when you get there. Remember: Self control is one of the most important tools a successful hunter uses to exceed at his sport. This is just as important in the sporting goods store as it is in the woods.

Finally, when you get your gear home, lay it all out and admire it. Check everything out thoroughly. If you bought new gear, try it on for size. Play with your new toys: You deserve it. I've always said that half the fun of hunting is in the preparations. You've done a good job planning your hunting trip, stayed within your budget, and you've purchased only what you need to have a safe and successful hunt. Savor it. It's part of the experience, and it's a lot of fun.

The Best Four Types of Hunting Stands

Besides your weapon, one of the biggest purchases you will make will be your hunting stand. When you get out into the woods, you want to be able to see the buck, but you don't want the buck to be able to see you. That's where hunting stands come into play.

Hunting stands are tools you use to hide from the deer. They include everything from elaborate shacks that are built up on stilts or in trees, to something as simple as a harness you can attach to a strong branch and hang on while you wait for your deer to approach.

Deer have highly developed senses of hearing, smell and sight. They can hear, see and smell you long before you can see them. One of the ways hunters overcome this advantage is by elevating themselves above the deer. In most cases, deer aren't looking for predators who are above them. Unless you are making a lot of noise, they won't see you if you are up in a stand.

There are four basic types of hunting stands. Which one you choose depends on your budget, where you are hunting, and what you prefer.

The first type of stand is called a ladder stand. This is basically a tall ladder with a small platform at the top that attaches to a tree. They are made for either one or two people. The advantage is that they are easy to climb and safe to sit in. They usually include a small rail you can use to steady your rifle. The disadvantage is that they are bulky to carry in and out of your hunting location. In most cases, they are hauled in by vehicle rather than carried in. This makes them impractical, if you are hunting on public land, and are not allowed to build semi-permanent structures. But, many people who hunt on private land will set up their ladder stands at the beginning of the hunting season and leave them up for the entire season, or even year round.

The second type of stand is called the climbing stand. This is a stand that is designed to fit on your back like a backpack, as you climb a steady tree. You can then mount the climbing stand onto the tree, and get into it to wait for your buck. The advantage is that they usually are very lightweight and portable, so it is easy to carry into and out of the hunting area during day hunts. This makes them perfect for hunting public lands. The disadvantage is that you have to be a little athletic in order to climb a tree wearing one, and then climb into the stand once you mount it. For hunters who are not in the best of shape or may be afraid of heights, they are perhaps not the best solution.

The third type of stand is called a hang-on stand. These are similar to climbing stands in that they are attached to a tree, but they are suspended either to a strong branch or the trunk using nylon ropes and clamps. Usually, they have a seat and a food rest. In some cases the seat is padded, which is highly beneficial, since you probably will be sitting in the stand for several hours as you wait for your buck to appear.

Finally, there is the tripod stand. These are used in areas where there aren't a lot of trees, or at least not trees big enough to support your weight. These semi-permanent structures feature a platform that rests on top of three or four legs, sort of like a giant stool. Obviously, you will need to install it long before the day of your hunt, so the deer can get used to it being there. As a result, you shouldn't use them on public land. They sometimes have a little roof to keep you out of the rain or snow, and are often camouflaged to keep the deer from seeing you.

Some hunters build permanent stands, if they are hunting on their own land. These are elevated structures made out of 2x4s and boards that are painted to be hidden from deer. In some cases, they are even heated.

If you don't want to use a stand, you can build your own blind out of downed trees or other debris. If you do this, make sure you clear an area inside where you can sit or stand without crunching leaves or sticks that the buck will hear. It is also helpful if you are elevated, so the buck can't see you.

There are also pop-up blinds you can buy, which can be set up in just a few moments, like an umbrella.

The disadvantage of hunting from a blind is that you are usually at ground level, so the deer can more easily smell and see you. Also, you have a narrower field of vision, so you won't have as many shot opportunities as you would from an elevated position.

Regardless of whether you use a stand or a blind, make sure you are comfortable, because in most cases you are going to be in there for several hours. Also, be aware of any noise you make. Every squeak, crunch and snap is like a cannon fire to a deer. Before you even get out in the woods, practice sitting very still and silent whenever you can, so that you will be better able to do so while hunting.

Deer Calls, Scents and Decoys

Deer may have better abilities to hear, smell and see than us, but we are smarter (or at least we like to think so). That's why deer calls, scents and decoys are such effective tools for attracting deer to your hunting location.

To the non-hunter, deer are silent animals that live their entire lives without uttering a sound. This is completely untrue. Deer communicate with each other all the time. Female deer warn their fawns of danger by bleating. Fawns bleat to let their mothers know their location.

Female deer will also bleat to attract males during mating season. This is called the Doe Estrus Bleat, and it is a highly effective way to attract a buck.

Bucks grunt to let other bucks know they are dominant and to mark their territory. They also grunt to challenge other males for supremacy. Bucks make a series of brief grunts directed at females during the mating season. This is called the Tending Grunt, and it tells the female deer that the male wants her to stand still, so that he can mount her.

Hunters learn to use these different types of deer calls during specific times throughout the hunt. For example, bleating like a fawn triggers a doe's maternal instinct, and she will usually come running, even if it is not her fawn. If there is a buck in hot pursuit of her, he will follow.

Using the Doe Estrus bleat can convince a buck that there is a doe in heat nearby, and he will come running toward the sound. And, aggressive grunts are a good way to attract mature bucks that are looking to establish their dominance with other bucks.

Scents are another great way to attract deer. You can buy natural and artificial deer scent to lure bucks to your hunting location. One of the most effective scents is the urine of a doe in heat. When you hang a bag of this urine from a tree in an area where you can get a clear shot during mating season, any buck in the area will naturally be attracted to it and will come looking for the doe.

Or, you can wipe the estrus urine of a doe on a tree trunk or branch, or dab it on a cloth and hang it from a tree branch to lure bucks into the open. Plus, when they finally arrive looking for a prospective mate, they will be confused and aroused, making them less cautious and giving the hunter an additional advantage.

You can also mask your own smell using cover scents to prevent the deer from locating you. Deer can easily smell the fragrances from your laundry detergents, soaps and shaving creams. It's a good idea to use fragrance free, hypo-allergenic detergents and soaps in the days and weeks leading up to the hunt, and invest in some masking scent to make you more invisible to the deer once you get into the woods.

Finally, deer decoys are an effective way to lure deer out into the open. When bucks see the decoy of another buck, their natural impulse is to challenge him, especially during the rutting season. Although deer will eventually realize that the decoy is not a real deer, it can take them long enough to reach that conclusion to meet their demise, as long as you have the opportunity for a clear shot.

You can add to the illusion by dabbing scent on the decoy, and by hanging a white cloth from its tail. Take extra care not to get your own scent on the decoy, or it won't fool the buck. Plus, it's a good idea to add a little blaze orange paint to your decoy to let other hunters know it's not a real deer, so they won't shoot at your decoy.

4 CHOOSE YOUR WEAPON: RIFLES, SHOTGUNS, PISTOLS, AND BOWS AND ARROWS

The type of weapon you use to hunt whitetail deer is dependent on where you live, the time of year, the type of hunting experience you are looking for, and your experience level as a hunter.

Different states have different hunting seasons. For example, in Wisconsin the seasons for hunting deer with rifles, bows and arrows, and muzzle-loaders are all different. Some states – such as Alaska and Texas – have longer seasons and fewer rules, while others – such as Illinois and Ohio – have relatively short hunting seasons and burden hunters with a lot of rules. Just for example, some states require hunters to wear a certain percentage of bright orange clothing, while others require a deer hunting education course as a prerequisite to getting a hunting license.

Hunting rifles are the best starting place for the new hunter, because they are relatively easy to use, and they allow you to shoot with high accuracy from a long distance away. As a result, they are a good choice for a hunter with less skill and experience.

Shotguns offer a great hunting experience, but can require more skill on the part of the hunter, because he or she has to get a lot closer to the deer in order to take it down.

Muzzle loading season is also typically a different season than rifle season, so it could be worth your while to purchase a muzzle loader, and learn how to use it. The upside is that they are usually a lot cheaper than hunting rifles. Participating in muzzle loading season will also give you more time to hunt. At the very least, you will have some additional scouting opportunities.

Pistols are not legal for deer hunting in all states, but if they are allowed where you live, they offer a deer hunting challenge. Handguns are generally less accurate, and have less range than a rifle. You will probably need to spend some time at the firing range to make sure you are comfortable and accurate with your weapon.

A bow and arrow provides a unique hunting experience. They don't have the range of a rifle, and shooting a bow and arrow with great accuracy takes a fair amount of practice to become proficient. It takes a lot of skill to kill a deer with a bow and arrow, and you don't want to take a shot if you are not certain the shot will kill the animal.

Bow hunting season usually starts earlier and lasts longer than rifle hunting season, so if you want first crack at the best bucks, you might consider learning how to shoot a bow and arrow. This will get you into the hunt earlier. Bringing down a big buck with only a bow and arrow is a huge thrill. But, the downside is that this is significantly more of a challenge.

Deer Hunting Rifles and Scopes: How to Choose the Right One for You

There are a lot of different kinds of deer hunting rifles, and they shoot different sized ammunition. On the small end are .22-caliber rifles. These are good for shooting small game, such as rabbits or possum, but are not powerful enough to dependably bring down a large deer. The rules vary by state, but rimfire rifles, such as the .22-caliber, are not legal to hunt deer with in Wisconsin, where I hunt.

On the opposite end of the spectrum are high caliber rifles. Many new hunters assume that the larger the caliber, the better the gun. This is not necessarily true for hunting deer. High caliber weapons can be more difficult to shoot, because their recoil is more powerful. This makes it difficult to stay in the relaxed state you need to be in to successfully hunt deer, if you're tensing up in anticipation of the recoil. Remember: You're just hunting deer, not grizzly bears.

There are also different kinds of hunting rifles: bolt action, lever action, single shot, and pump action. Give yourself enough time to learn the benefits and drawbacks of each. Ask a lot of questions at the gun store. The salesmen will be happy to help you out.

Another thing to keep in mind, is that you want to buy a gun you can easily buy ammunition for. If you get a fancy gun with an unusual caliber, you are more limited than if you buy a gun you can buy ammunition for at your closest sporting goods store.

You will also want to buy a rifle that fits you. Rifles come in all different sizes. If you are a big guy, you are going to need a bigger gun. If you are smaller, look at rifles with shorter stocks and barrels. While there is no rule of thumb, pick up a lot of different rifles and see how they feel. You will know if they are too big or too small.

More deer probably have been shot with the good old 30-30 than any other rifle. They've proven to be very popular over the years and many hunters, including myself, began hunting with them when they were kids. Even if you don't own one, you probably know someone who does, and they would be more than happy to let you try it out.

Another good all-purpose rifle is the .270-caliber Winchester. It has a high level of accuracy, good range, and it's a good caliber for hunting whitetail deer. It has enough power, but not so big it's going to knock you on your rear end or give you a sore shoulder for the rest of the day. The .270 Winchester gives you a high level of accuracy from 100 to 250 yards, which should give you plenty of range for whitetail deer.

Another popular caliber for deer hunting is the 30-06. It has plenty of knock-down power and good range.

Any rifle, when properly fired, has the capability of taking down a deer. In the end you'll have to decide which rifle you like shooting best and are the most comfortable with.

You can buy your deer rifle either new or used. Obviously, a new rifle right out of the display case is going to cost more, but you will have the satisfaction of knowing that it has never been fired and is in perfect condition. Plus, it will usually come with a money back guarantee, if something is wrong with it or maybe even if you don't like it. With a used weapon, you take the chance that it has been worn or damaged, but you will spend less money. Remember to check the bore for rust and pitting.

When it comes to buying a rifle scope, you should look for the best scope that you can afford. There are scopes available for as little as $30 to $40, but remember, you get what you pay for.

The most common scope on hunting rifles is 3x-9x, which means what you are looking at is magnified between 3 times and 9 times. The 40mm objective lens is the most common. For a good scope, you can expect to spend between $130 and $200. Look for ones with a matte finish, so your scope isn't a shiny distraction to your buck when you get out in the woods.

Also, look for scopes that fit low on the rifle and are durable. They are likely going to get beat up a little while you are tramping around the woods, so you don't want a delicate one that is going to break easily. Different scopes have different types of cross hairs you see, when you look through them while aiming, so find the one that you like the best.

Shotguns, Pistols and other Firearms

Shotguns are literally a blast to fire, but they come in all different sizes and types. For deer hunting, you're going to want to use slugs. There are four basic types of shotguns.

The first is the single shot shotgun, which holds only one shell at a time. They are typically the least expensive option, are great for beginners, and safer for younger hunters, because there is only one shot in the chamber.

The second type is the pump action shotgun. This is the most popular type. They hold multiple shells, and require you to pump the fore-end to eject the spent shell and load a new shell into the chamber. They are very reliable and fall into the low to mid price range, depending on the model you select.

A semi-automatic shotgun will eject the shell and load a new shell into the chamber automatically. Not only are these more efficient, but they have about 30 percent less recoil than pump action or single shot shotguns, because the automatic cycling action absorbs some of the recoil. They are generally more expensive, however.

The final shotgun type is the double barrel shotgun. It holds two shells at a time, and comes in either an over/under or side-by-side style. They usually have a shorter barrel than pump action or semi-automatic shotguns, and you can crack them open to see if there are rounds in the chamber, making them safer. Double barrel shotguns are very reliable, but they also tend to be the most expensive.

Shotguns come in a variety of barrel sizes, but the most common are 12, 16 and 20 gauge. The larger the bore, the bigger the kick a shotgun will have. For deer, you probably will want a larger bore shotgun with easy to use sights. Larger bore shotguns produce more recoil, so keep that in mind when picking out your shotgun.

When picking out a pistol, you need to consider whether you want a revolver or a semi-automatic. With a revolver, the casing from a fired charge stays in the slot and the barrel is turned when you pull the trigger, placing a fresh round in front of the firing pin. With a semi-automatic, a spring mechanism ejects spent casing and the forces a new round into the chamber. It takes more strength to pull the trigger on a revolver, while a semi-automatic has a lighter trigger.

Again, handguns come in all different size gauges. Smaller gauge pistols, such as a .22-caliber, generally are not used for deer hunting. Very large gauges, such as a .44 Magnum, are a lot of fun to shoot, but tend to be heavier to carry. They also carry a pretty good kick. Look for a mid-range gauge handgun – such as a 9mm semi-automatic or a .38-caliber revolver. In the end, however, it's a matter of personal preference.

Muzzle loaded rifles are another challenging weapon for hunting deer. These are the old fashioned rifles in which you load powder and shot down the muzzle of the gun, and then tamp it down with a ramrod. You normally only get one shot at a deer when you're using a muzzleloader, as you need to wait for the barrel to cool for at least a minute before reloading. Most muzzleloaders are equipped with open sights, though some of the more modern ones can be equipped with a scope.

Muzzleloaders often have special hunting seasons, so you could increase your hunting time if you hunt these seasons. Rules vary greatly by state, so be sure to check your local regulations.

Under the category of bow and arrow, there are many different types of bows. For the beginner, the compound bow will be the easiest to learn on and to handle. Compound bows have a mechanical setup, which makes it easier to hold back the string once it is drawn back. They also shoot arrows flatter. Recurve, or single string bows, are more difficult to use, and shoot arrows with more of an arc. Regardless of which type of bow and arrow setup you choose, make sure you practice a lot before heading out for your hunt.

When purchasing arrows, make sure you buy ones that are compatible with your bow. Not every arrow can be used on every bow. For a modern compound bow, you're going to want to use aluminum arrows or carbon shaft arrows. They won't shatter or split, unlike wood, so they are safer.

5 GUN SAFETY: THE ESSENTIALS

Hunting with weapons is fun and exciting. But, it is also potentially dangerous. About 1,000 people are injured each year in hunting accidents, and about 100 of those are killed. Rifles, shotguns, handguns, cross bows, bows and arrows, and even hunting knives are dangerous weapons, and need to be treated with the respect they deserve.

Most gun safety rules are just common sense, but it's important to review them regularly to avoid hunting accidents. Many states require people to complete a certified gun safety course prior to being issued a hunting license or get a Firearm Owners Identification card.

You should always wear eye and ear protection, as appropriate. And, you should never use a gun, if you have been drinking alcohol or have taken prescription or other drugs. Make sure you store your guns in a manner in which they are not accessible to unauthorized persons, especially children.

While hunting, never point a gun at anybody, loaded or unloaded. It's a good idea to always assume a gun is loaded, even if you are certain that it is not. It only takes being wrong one time to cause a tragedy. If you assume a gun is loaded, you will always make sure it is pointed in a safe direction. This means that even if the gun were to go off, it would not hurt anybody or damage anything. The key is keep the barrel pointed in a safe direction at all times. For example, when you are walking to your hunting spot, hold your rifle so that the barrel is pointed at the ground or directly up in the air, even when you are climbing over logs or rocks.

Many, if not most, accidental shootings occur because the shooter thought the gun wasn't loaded. For example, if a gun has no magazine in it, someone might assume it is not able to fire. But, there can easily be a round in the chamber even if there is no magazine. Or, perhaps someone hands you a gun and tells you it is not loaded. Unless you double-check yourself, there is no way you can say with 100 percent certainty that there is nothing in the chamber. Similarly, even if the safety is on, a gun can sometimes still fire due to mechanical failure.

Make sure you keep your finger off the trigger until you are ready to shoot. This includes the time you spend in your stand or behind your blind. Wait until the last possible moment before you put your finger on the trigger. You can be just as prepared if you rest your finger on your trigger guard or alongside your gun. Many guns have hair triggers, meaning even the slightest pressure can fire them. If you keep your finger off your trigger until the moment you are ready to shoot, you can prevent an accidental discharge.

Don't load your weapon until you are ready to use it. Usually, this means when you get into your stand or behind your blind. It's unlikely you're going to come across a trophy buck as you are tramping through the woods to your hunting spot. Preventing an accidental shooting is more important than the one in a million chance that you will turn a corner to find your trophy buck standing there. Even if you are sure your gun is not loaded, always keep the safety device on, remove any magazine and check the chamber to make sure there is not a round left in it. If you are not sure how to open your gun, ask somebody who knows to show you.

A Beginner's Guide to Firearms Safety: Before You Buy Your Gun

Gun safety is one of the most important topics to consider when preparing for your hunt. If you are involved in a hunting accident, either as the shooter or the victim, it can negatively impact your life forever. It is better to spend some time reviewing the proper way to handle weapons ahead of time. It doesn't take a long time, and the lessons you learn will make your experience a lot better and safer.

Basic gun safety rules are available online at the NRA's website. Another option is to enroll in a gun safety course in your area. You can find one close to you, online or by asking your gun retailer or law enforcement office to recommend a course. They are generally one-day courses that cover everything you need to know before you head out on your hunt, so you can have a fun yet safe hunting experience. In some states, gun safety courses are a prerequisite to getting a hunting license or deer tags.

When considering buying a weapon, ask your salesperson about all of its safety features. Where is the safety located and how does it work? How do you check to see if there is a round in the chamber? Does it come with an external gun guard? Can you store the clip and the gun separately? Does it come with a lockable case?

Before you buy a gun, find out how it works. The salesperson at your firearms store will be happy to explain the mechanics of any weapon they sell. In fact, once you get them started it's sometimes hard to shut them up! But, understanding how your rifle or handgun operates will only help you operate it more safely, and keep it functioning correctly for as long as you own it.

Before you bring a weapon into your home, think about where you are going to store it. Many people like to have access to a weapon in their home for personal safety, but keeping a loaded gun under your pillow or in a holster hanging from your bed post is just asking for trouble. A better idea would be to invest in a lockable gun safe that you can easily access in case of trouble. This will keep unauthorized persons – such as your children or burglars – from gaining access to your guns, while still allowing you to get to them fast when you want them.

Guns are fascinating to children, and special care needs to be taken in households where kids live. You don't want to be the one explaining to police why your child brought a loaded weapon to show and tell at their school, and you certainly don't want to have an accidental shooting in your home. You can enjoy hunting, and still be smart about storing guns securely in your home.

Consider how you plan to control your gun while you are traveling to and from your hunting site, both in your vehicle and in the woods. Many states require hunters to store weapons in the trunk of their vehicle, unloaded and in a locking case. While you are walking to and from your stand or blind, you might consider keeping your gun in its case until you get there. It's safer and will protect your weapon from getting nicked and dinged on trees and rocks.

Avoiding Accidents: Deadly Errors Even Veteran Hunters Can Make

The first mistake many hunters make is failing to properly maintain their guns.

Guns are mechanical tools with a lot of moving parts. As such, they require regular maintenance in order to operate correctly. Learn how to take your gun apart, and put it back together. Learn the names of all the parts, and how they function. And, most important of all, learn how to clean and maintain your weapon for maximum efficiency. If there is something wrong with your gun, make sure you bring it to a gunsmith, so he can make the necessary repairs.

Your gun needs to be cleaned every time you use it. Residue from the gunpowder can build up in your chamber and barrel, and cause your gun to shoot inaccurately, or even cause your weapon to misfire. Taking care of your gun will also extend its life and maintain its value.

If you haven't fired your gun in a long time, make sure you clean it before shooting it. Moisture and dirt can accumulate within your gun, as can solidified grease and oil. These will prevent your gun from firing properly, so they need to be removed.

Finally, before cleaning your gun, always make sure it is not loaded. Never look down the barrel of any gun. When cleaning your gun, make sure the action is open throughout the cleaning process, and there is no ammunition anywhere near your weapon.

The second mistake even many veteran hunters make is failing to take into account what may be behind their targets. Rifle bullets travel at a very fast speed and for a very long distance, sometimes as much as a mile. If you miss your mark, that bullet is going to keep going until it strikes something or runs out of speed. Even if you strike your mark, the bullet can still pass through your target and hit something or somebody else.

Never fire in a direction where there may be people or anything that could be damaged by your shot. Observing your prospective area before you fire will help prevent accidents. Make sure nothing is moving in front of your target that could be hit by your bullet.

Spending a lot of time at the shooting range taking target practice will improve your chances of not hitting anything except your intended target. In many cases, as a hunter you will only have one shot at your target, so you will want to make sure you spend the time improving your precision as you get ready for that moment. Plus, getting familiar with your weapon and interacting with it is half the fun of being a gun owner.

A third mistake that is made a lot is drinking while hunting. I understand that a lot of times hunting is something you do with your buddies. When you get out into the woods, it's a time to have fun and enjoy yourself, and to appreciate the time you spend away from the worries of your daily life. I also get that it can be really cold sitting in your stand or behind your blind waiting for your trophy buck to turn the corner, and a little nip from a bottle can help you keep the cold at bay for a little while. But, the fact of the matter is that when you are hunting, you are handling a dangerous weapon. When you are drinking, it's easier to make a mistake. Even after drinking a small amount of alcohol, your senses can become impaired, and your reaction time is slowed down. There will be plenty of time to have a few beers with your friends when the day is done, but any time you have access to loaded weapons that have deadly force is not the time to take alcohol or party.

Exhaustion is another form of impairment, so if you have been sleep deprived or are physically exhausted, your ability to handle a weapon accurately and safely will be impacted.

Finally, the last mistake even veteran hunters sometimes make is ignoring secondary dangers. These include the noise caused by firing a gun close to your eardrum, the hot gases and shells that are ejected from your weapon when you fire it, and ricochets of bullets fired against hard surfaces, such as rocks or ironwoods.

If you are hunting with a gun you have never used before, it may have a louder report or recoil than you are used to. This can be a problem, if you are sitting in a stand high up in a tree. Make sure you know how the gun is going to react before you fire it, otherwise you may find yourself falling out of a tree rather than bagging your trophy buck.

Also, understand your physical limitations. If you are in the best shape of your life and can hike 20 miles easily through rugged terrain, more power to you. But, if you live a sedentary lifestyle and don't make to the gym as often as you should, don't try to do too much once you get out into the woods. A lot of times, the best hunting grounds are a long way away from the nearest medical center or even cell phone signal, so help may not be as close as you would like, if something were to go wrong. Take it easy and understand your limits.

How to Ensure a Safe and Enjoyable Hunting Experience for Everybody

Hunting is a fun experience that can be enjoyed by people of any age or background. Creating an exciting and safe hunting experience is easy, if you keep a few simple things in mind.

While you may think it looks cool to get dressed up in your best camouflage clothes and blend seamlessly into the woods, rendering yourself invisible to your quarry, remember that it makes you invisible to other hunters, as well. Wearing bright orange clothing, or including some bright orange markings on your hunting gear is something I personally have resisted for many years, but now see the benefit. It only takes one accident to change somebody's life, so take it from me that it's more important to be visible to other hunters than it is to be invisible to deer. In most cases, you are going to be up in your stand or behind your blind, so the deer won't be looking at you anyway.

Let somebody know where you are going and what time you will be back. Check the weather before you leave to make sure you don't get caught in something severe. Also, make sure you have the proper clothing to respond to rapid changes in the weather. Nothing ruins a hunting trip like getting caught in a downpour without wet weather gear.

Some hunting guides recommend never hunting alone. This is a hard one for me, because a lot of time I prefer to hunt by myself. Better advice would be never to hunt alone when you are first starting out. Hunting with an experienced companion will not only keep you safer, but will also teach you hunting tips and techniques that would probably take a long time to figure out on your own. No matter how many guidebooks, websites and videos you look at, the experience of actually being out in the woods with your hunting gear is going to be different than you imagined it. You can make it even better by starting out learning under the guidance of somebody who knows what they are talking about.

Check, double check and triple check your equipment before you head out, even if it is brand new. The moment you are climbing up into your stand is the wrong time to find out that you forgot your clamps. Walk through your entire hunt from start to finish, before you ever leave your home. Make sure you have everything you need, and that it works the way it is supposed to. Your weapon is the most important thing, but even little things like extra socks or toilet paper can make or break your hunting trip in certain situations. Take the time and get it right before you start.

Most importantly, have fun. Hunting is a great experience that will teach you a lot about nature, as well as about yourself. Savor every moment of the experience. Being that close to nature is something that doesn't happen to us enough. Keep your eyes open to what is happening around you. This will help you bring the right attitude that will make your hunting experience something you can cherish for the rest of your life.

6 HOW NOT TO GET LOST IN THE WOODS (AND WHAT TO DO IF IT HAPPENS)

Deer hunting can take you to some pretty remote places. Whether you are hunting on private land or public space, when you are tracking your deer it's easy to get disoriented and stop paying attention to where you are. On the best hunting trips, you will know ahead of time exactly where you want to set up your stand to wait for your deer. But, even then, it is easy to get lost, if you are not experienced in moving through the woods.

This is where spending time studying topographical maps, and scouting your deer hunting locations pay off. The more time you spend planning your hunt, the more familiar you become with the area where you will be hunting. You can learn what landmarks to look for and where they will be located by carefully reviewing a detailed map of the area where you will be hunting.

Hunting is a year-round activity. During the off-season, the best hunters are spending time scouting the woods, and looking for the areas with the highest likelihood of finding bucks during hunting season. Getting familiar with the lay of the land during the off-season will help you when you are on your hunt.

The best way to avoid getting lost in the woods is by only hunting in areas that you are intimately familiar with. A lot of hunters go back to the same hunting spots year after year, so they get to know what landmarks to look for, and how to find their way in and out of the brush. Even in these cases, you can still get horribly lost while you are tracking your deer. Once you have shot it, in most cases, your deer will take off. As you follow your deer deeper and deeper into the woods, you can take all kinds of turns, so it's easy to get turned around. Many hunters have finally caught up with their deer only to discover that they have no idea where the hell they are.

The best tool you have against getting lost in the woods is preparation. Maps, scouting trips and just common sense are enough for most people to find their way out of unfamiliar areas. But, when these things fail, there are some other tools you can use to help you find your way home.

True North: GPS, Smart Phones and Topographical Maps

A simple compass is one of the best tools you can have to keep yourself oriented. The way a compass works is that magnetized pointers float freely, allowing them to align with the earth's magnetic field, which runs north to south. When you look at a compass, it will point north.

You can purchase an inexpensive compass for just a few dollars at any sporting goods store, and you should always carry one while hunting. There's even a free app you can download to your smart phone that will point you toward true north.

When you start your journey into the woods, take a look at your compass. Determine which general direction you will be traveling: north, south, east or west. Then, determine which direction the main road is in relation to your direction of travel. For example, if you are hiking north, the road you drove in on is south of where you will be walking. Orienting yourself to where you started lets you use your compass to find your way out, if you become lost or disoriented.

Leave a note on the dashboard of your vehicle stating that you are hunting in the woods, date it and give your estimated time and date of return. That way, if you somehow become lost, and somebody finds your vehicle, they will know that you have missed your deadline. They will be able to notify the authorities, so that they can launch a search party for you.

It's a good idea to have a topographical map of the area in which you will be hunting. Maps are available online and at the forestry service office in the area where you will be hunting. These maps show not only major landmarks – roads, rivers and streams – but they also show changes in elevation, so you can tell where the land is rising and falling. The closer the elevation lines are on the map, the steeper the altitude change.

If you are going into an unknown area of the woods, make a mark on your topographical map the location where your vehicle is located. Then, make another mark on the hunting site where you will be setting up your stand. Finally, plan your route from your vehicle location to your hunting site, taking the path of least resistance – in other words, no crossing rivers, climbing steep inclines or navigating murky swamps. Carry your map with you as you make your way to your hunting site.

Smart phones have Global Positioning Systems (GPS) built into them. These allow you to orient yourself from anywhere based on satellites that hang above the earth in geo-synchronous orbit. So, the first thing you will want to do if you become lost is look at your smart phone to see if you have a signal. If you have a signal, all you need to do is open up the map application and find out where you are. Then, follow the route back to your vehicle.

Because there aren't a lot of cell phone towers in the deep woods and the range of cell phone antennas is limited, a lot of the time you won't be able to take advantage of the simple solution.

The Lessons of Hansel and Gretel: Marking Your Route

In the old fairy tale, Hansel and Gretel marked their route through the dense woods by leaving a trail of bread crumbs. But, they became lost after the woods creatures ate their bread crumbs, and the siblings couldn't find their way out of the woods.

Okay, maybe leaving a trail of bread crumbs was a pretty stupid idea, but you can mark your route just like the fabled Hansel and Gretel in a number of different ways.

First, you can purchase a GPS device that will tell you where you are from anywhere on the globe, and it does not require being within range of a cell phone tower.

These are becoming increasingly affordable, and most even include downloadable topographical maps. Most of the devices will set the electronic equivalent of bread crumbs every couple of minutes, so you will always know exactly where you are and where you have been.

Generally, GPS devices will work, even when there is dense cloud or tree cover. But, if your GPS is not working, or you didn't bring a GPS and you are out of range of a cell phone tower, you can still mark your route by using your smart phone to take pictures of landmarks along your route. Simply snap a photo every 30 minutes, or at every major landmark, such as a river or stream or fork in the trail, and make a notation on your map of where you are. That way, if you get turned around, you can just compare the photos to the landmarks to determine if you are going in the right direction.

Just make sure your cell phone is charged, before you head out. You don't want to have the thing die on you just when you need it the most. Depending on the model and how much you use it, cell phones generally will hold a charge for at least 24 hours. Charging it in your vehicle as you drive to your hunting site is recommended.

Finally, if all else fails, you can use the old school way of marking your trail. Some people bring along brightly colored marking ribbons. You can find these at most sporting goods stores. Attach them to trees or shrubs every 50 yards or so. Even though this is probably not going to hurt anything, it does change the woods just a little for future users, preventing them from having the same pristine experience that you are enjoying. So, if you are not going to remove them all on your way out, it's not recommended.

Instead, break off low-hanging twigs and branches from trees and shrubs along your route to give yourself a sign that this was the area you traveled through. You can leave a sign every 25 yards or so, or as often as you want. Just remember to always try to use the same sign, such as a branch broken in half, but not detached from the tree. Don't do too much damage, such as pulling out shrubs or overturning small trees or rock piles. Leaving a trail of environmentally-friendly signs doesn't harm the environment, and provides you with a clear sign of the path you traveled.

Don't Panic: A Field Guide to Finding Your Way Out

Sometimes, even though we've tried to do everything right, it all goes wrong. If you find yourself hopelessly lost in the woods, you can't communicate with anybody, and you have no tools to find your way out, the most important thing you can do is to stay calm. Panicking will only exhaust your strength, and will not help you solve your problem. Instead, sit down, take some deep breaths and listen.

Your hearing is the first tool you have at your disposal to finding your way out of the woods. Listen for the sounds of cars, trucks or trains. Listen for the sound of airplanes flying over head. Listen for the rifle shots of other hunters. All of these things can help you find your way out.

For example, if you hear rifle shots, move toward them. The hunters who are firing those guns, in all likelihood, know how to get back to their vehicles, so they can help you.

If you hear the sounds of car or truck engines, you can make your way to a road where you can flag somebody down who can help you. If you hear a train, you can find a rail line that you can follow, until you reach a town. You might have to hike a ways, but it's better than staying put in the woods.

Don't try to make your way out of the woods in the dark. Even if there is a full moon, it won't be enough light to prevent you from tripping over a root, falling down an incline or otherwise injuring yourself. A better idea is to make camp for the night, and wait for first light.

Building a fire is important, because the woods can get very cold at night, even during the summer. Also, a fire will signal your position, and will keep predators away. You should always bring waterproof matches with you, when you travel into the woods, but if you don't have matches or a lighter, you can start a fire with glasses or the old-fashioned way by creating a friction lighter with a couple of sticks and some kindling.

Finding a fresh water supply is also a priority. While humans can survive for weeks without food, dehydration can kill you in only a few days. Fortunately, most forests have plentiful fresh water supplies.

Don't eat any berries, nuts or any other food you find in the woods, even if you think you know it is safe. There are many toxic plants and fruits in the woods that can cause you to hallucinate, shut down your internal organs, and even kill you! If you must eat something, shoot some small game, and cook it over your fire. Don't eat animals you find already dead, however, because they contain billions of bacteria that can make you sick and may even kill you.

Getting out of the woods as quickly as possible needs to be a priority. You can quickly begin to starve, if you don't have enough food, even if you are able to hunt occasional small game. The amount of food you will be eating is far less than what your body is accustomed to. So, your body will quickly begin to weaken, and your energy level will start to decline.

7 PLANNING THE HUNT: WHAT TO CONSIDER BEFORE HEADING OUT

Once you start getting into hunting, it will become obvious to you that your interest in hunting is not just something you indulge during the deer hunting season. It is a year round activity. Throughout the year, hunters love to follow their sport by reading hunting magazines or visiting some of the dozens of websites devoted to the sport.

Off season is also the time to scout next season's best hunting locations, planning where to put your stand or blind, and watching the deer population, so you can learn from its patterns the best places to hunt.

You can perfect your marksmanship throughout the year by scheduling time at the firing range. Make sure you bring all the weapons you plan to use on your hunt, and that you thoroughly clean your weapons after every shooting session, so they perform to optimum efficiency.

When you are not practicing your shooting, another thing to practice is being quiet. When you climb into your stand during your hunting trip, you may need to remain silent for several hours, while you wait for your trophy buck to appear. This is easier said than done. Try to keep still for increasingly longer periods of time, until you are confident you can remain perfectly motionless, when the time comes for your actual hunt.

Avid hunters are always thinking about what new rifles they want to buy, or improving their scopes. Getting accustomed to new equipment is something that should be done during the off season, not right before the hunt. You never want to go into the woods with equipment that you are not entirely familiar with.

The same thing applies to your hunting clothes. Deer will smell brand new clothes a mile away (actually, maybe even further). Be sure to wash your new hunting clothes with scent free detergent without UV brighteners.

If you are hunting on private land and are planning to build a deer stand, the earlier you can build it the better. That's because it takes deer a while to get used to anything new in their environment. If you give them a couple of weeks, or even months, to become accustomed to having this new structure in their habitat, it will be all but invisible to them by the time hunting season rolls around. Plus, it may be necessary to haul in the equipment and building supplies by vehicle, which may chase off any deer that may be in the area.

If you are hunting on private land, always get the permission of the landowner in writing ahead of time. Be prepared to pay a fee. Also, be aware that in the country, country rules apply. If you trespass on someone's land without permission, not only could you get hurt, but the local law may side with the landowner. Once you get permission, however, hunting on private land can be a better way to go, because it probably won't be over-hunted. You are unlikely to run into a lot of other hunting parties, and the owner can probably steer you toward the most effective places to set up your stand.

You can even ask the landowner if he or she would be willing to let you visit the property in the months leading up to the hunt, so you can scout the best locations, set up your stand, and get to learn the lay of the land. As long as you are not intrusive, in many cases, they will allow it. In addition, once you build a relationship with the owner of some good hunting land, you can return there year after year.

The weeks leading up to the hunting season can be particularly busy, so you don't want to wait until the last minute to do preparations that could be done long ahead of time. In the weeks before hunting season begins, you will be busy making sure you have your license and deer tags, double-checking your equipment, resupplying those items you will need, and talking to fellow hunters about the best places to go and what you can expect from the woods this season. Getting ready for the hunt is almost as fun and exciting as the hunting itself!

Don't forget to tell someone your hunting plan. Let somebody know where you are going, how long you will be there, and the latest time they should expect you back before calling the authorities. If you are hunting with other hunters, meet up at least once before your trip to talk about the hunt, and how you plan to execute it. Decide who is going to be responsible for what equipment. Come up with a plan, in case you become separated. Swap stories about previous hunts and brag about how big of a trophy buck you are going to be bringing back.

Reading the Moon and Weather Patterns

When you talk to most hunters, they will tell you about the way the moon influences where and how deer move through the woods. Some theorize that the rut begins exactly two weeks after the first full moon, after the fall equinox. Others will tell you deer move more frequently during the low light phases of the moon.

While the light that is reflected off of the moon may influence the way deer behave, the stage of the moon itself has not been proven to have any effect whatsoever. While the amount of light available for feeding plays a role in deer migration, it is only one of many factors that influence where and when deer move from one area to another. Other things to consider are where the food supply is the largest, how many predators have been in the area, the direction of the wind, and whether or not it's hunting season.

The amount of light the moon provides determines whether deer will be feeding or not. During the new moon phase, when there is no light, deer will stay hidden and not feed, because they cannot see the food supply, and they can't see predators. When the moon is in its waxing and waning phases, there is partial light from the moon. Deer will venture out to feed, but are not as active as when there is a full moon and maximum light.

Similarly, the amount of daylight plays a central role in deer social life. Scientists now say the rut begins when the amount of daylight decreases to a specific level, as fall turns to winter. Deer can sense the days are getting shorter, and this triggers the desire to reproduce before winter sets in. It's no coincidence that hunting season in most states coincides with the rut, which is slightly different everywhere, but generally occurs between the first weeks of autumn and the first weeks of winter.

Male deer in search of mates become less cautious, and will wander out of their regular feeding grounds. They respond more aggressively to the grunts of competing bucks, and will sometimes rush into a clearing, if they think there is a chance to demonstrate their dominance over another animal.

Weather patterns also play a major role in deer behavior. During the warm summer months, whitetail prefer to feed at first daylight, and again just after the sun goes down. During the hottest part of the day, they prefer to gather in the cooler, shadier areas of the woods.

As temperatures fall during the autumn months, feeding deer will stay out for longer periods of time during the day. And, in the cold winter months, when the temperature reaches zero degrees and below, deer will seek out sunny spots where they can conserve energy and stay warm. In winter, they will also feed from morning and mid-afternoon, because they need to find more food in order to maintain their energy levels. At this time, there is less food available.

If the weather is windy, deer prefer not to move very far, because it makes it difficult for them to smell predators. Similarly, in severe rain or snow deer will not wander far from their bedding areas, preferring the comfort and security of their homes. They are perfectly fine with feeding during light rain or snow, however.

Deer will sense changes in weather patterns long before you will. They have the ability to sense changes to barometric pressure. If there is a storm approaching, deer will generally move ahead of it, toward their bedding areas. A full 8 to 16 hours before bad weather patterns emerge, deer will bed down. They generally won't leave until the weather clears, and they can return to feeding.

In the days leading up to your hunt, you will want to pay close attention to the weather patterns in the area you will be hunting. Also, consider the stages of the moon on the days leading up to and during your hunt. Finally, try to find out if the rut has begun, and if so, how long it has been going on. If the rut is in full swing, online message boards will be blazing with hunters exchanging information with each other.

By studying the weather and moonlight in your hunting area in the days leading up to your hunt and while you are at your hunting site, you can tell you a lot about how the deer in your hunting area are going to behave once you arrive there.

Where the Deer Are: Scouting Optimal Hunting Locations

In most cases, hunters know way ahead of time where they will be hunting when the deer season begins. This gives them plenty of time to scout the best locations for their stands. Scouting hunting grounds can begin as early as the spring, as hunters head to the woods to start looking for deer movements and patterns.

When scouting hunting locations, you should use as much caution as possible. When you enter a deer's territory, they can sense your presence. In most cases, they will see you long before you spot them. Try to scout from a distance using a pair of high-powered binoculars, whenever possible. Stay downwind from the area you are scouting, so the deer can't smell you. Scout during the early morning and late afternoon hours with the sun behind you, to minimize the chance of being spotted.

You are looking for trails deer use to move from their beds to feeding and watering grounds; water supplies that are used by a lot of deer; locations which are optimal for deer to feed on, such as breaks between dense woods and open fields with good food sources; and deer herds themselves. Look for heavily traveled trails leading from the woods into the field. Deer prefer to enter areas from the corners, not from directly on, to minimize their exposure to predators. Check the corners of fields and clearings first.

Fresh deer scat and urine is a good indicator that deer have recently been in an area. Especially, look for deer feces near water supplies, such as rivers and streams. Deer droppings are dark and moist when fresh, and tightly clustered and oval. The droppings are effective clues in tracking your quarry.

Deer will drink throughout the day, but they almost always hit their water supply first thing in the morning and right before sundown. So, these are prime scouting times near watering holes. Even if you don't spot deer, if you find fresh dung, you have probably discovered a prime location for your deer hunting.

Scrutinize feeding areas for signs: hoof prints, soft, fresh droppings, chewed apples on abandoned orchards, soybean fields with plants stripped of leaves, alfalfa fields with bender tops chewed off. Look for food sources that deer love, such as apple trees and the acorns from white oaks. These are especially popular areas after a rainstorm, because deer are anxious to start feeding again. Interestingly, deer prefer fresh acorns to ones that have been on the ground for awhile. Pay attention to the trees, so you can spot the ones that are dropping a lot of acorns.

While whitetail deer adore the acorns from white oaks, they are much more discerning when it comes to acorns from red oaks. You will need to learn how to tell the difference between the two trees. White oaks can be a deer hunter's best friend, but red oaks can be a waste of your time, especially if there are white oaks in the area.

Finally, deer will change their behavior patterns, as hunting season progresses. You are more likely to find them where you expect them earlier in the season rather than later. As the season progresses, however, the rut begins, and everything is up for grabs. Mature males and females start to go crazy as they look for mating partners.

Top Ten Ways to Guarantee a Successful Hunt

If you ask 12 hunters for their top 10 tips to guaranteeing a successful hunt, you will get 12 completely different lists. Everybody has their own techniques that have worked for them, so I have tried to compile a list of the most common tips that any hunter can use to improve his or her chances of bagging a trophy buck. These are in no particular order.

1. **Your personal safety is the most important thing during any hunt** – Whether it is

gun safety, wearing a harness when sitting in your tree stand, or being aware of where you are in the woods so you don't get lost, there is no better way to ruin a hunt than by having an accident. Always keep the safety of yourself and other hunters in the forefront of your mind at all times, and you will have many fun, enjoyable hunting experiences.

2. **Always be ethical and follow hunting etiquette** – Make sure you know what the hunting laws are in the area where you are hunting and that you have the proper licenses, deer tags and stamps. Don't hunt on private land without permission, and don't violate the hunting rules when hunting on public land. You can get in a lot of trouble, and you will only make it worse for other hunters later.

3. **Buy the best equipment that you can afford and take care of it** – Hunting rifles, clothing and other gear are available in a whole

range of prices. Try to find the equipment that works best for you and falls within your budget. Then, take care of your equipment, so it will take care of you when you are out in the woods.

4. **Be open to learning from other hunters** – Even the best hunters are open to the ideas and suggestions of others. Interact with others within the hunting community. Learn from their mistakes and successes. There is an endless amount of information to know about hunting whitetail deer. Keeping an open mind will only make you a better hunter.

5. **Have respect for nature** – When you shoot a deer, be respectful of the fact that it is another living creature. Hunting is not about shooting animals for fun. It's about the experience of being closer to nature, providing food for your family, helping control the deer population, and being a better person. Try to minimize your impact on the natural world, when you are in the

woods. They have been there long before you were even born, and they will be there long after you are gone.

6. **Be a student of nature** – Every time you go into the woods, you have the opportunity to learn something new about your sport, the behavior of whitetail deer, and the way the natural world works. Pay attention, because the deer will teach you how to become a better hunter and a better person.

7. **Practice self control** – Whether you are sitting in your stand waiting for your buck to appear, or sitting at your home or office during the off months waiting for deer season to begin, practice the self-control skills you will need to be the best hunter you can possibly be. Like anything else, the more you practice, the more skilled you will become.

8. **Become a marksman** – Probably the biggest mistake new hunters make is that they think they are better shooters than they actually are. In many cases, you will have only one opportunity to take down your buck, after waiting long hours in your stand. Make the most of that opportunity by putting in the time at the firing range to improve your shooting skills.

9. **Be aware** – Whenever you are in the woods, always try to keep the sun at your back, and stay downwind of where you think your prey will be. Be aware of the noise you are making and of how you are moving. Walking slowly, focusing on your movements and pay attention to how the deer perceive you will only help you to be a better hunter.

10. **Mix it up** – Don't always hunt from the same stand. Don't always hunt from a stand. Try different hunting techniques, such as still hunting, spot and stalk, and deer drives. Just because a

technique worked for you once doesn't mean it is always the best solution for the current situation. Trying different hunting techniques will only improve your chances.

8 THE IMPORTANCE OF SCENT CONROL

Deer have a sense of smell that is a thousand times more sensitive than a human's. A deer can smell you long before it can see you, and certainly long before you can see him. One of the biggest mistakes new hunters make is not taking into consideration the way they smell. While it is one thing to position yourself so that you are always downwind from the deer, the expert hunter also seeks to control the way deer perceive him or her through the deer's enhanced sense of smell.

A deer's sense of smell is even more sensitive than a dog's. They can detect the odor of predators from hundreds of yards away. It is one of their primary defense mechanisms, because deer rely on their excellent sense of smell for survival.

The deer's sense of smell combines with their excellent hearing to give them an awareness in the woods that is much more advanced than ours. As you scout your deer, watch the way their moist noses are constantly twitching. That means they are scanning the air drafts for scents they associate with danger. Their noses are twitching, even when they are feeding.

If a deer detects something, it will stop what it is doing and lift its head up. Watch its ears. A deer's ears have the ability to pivot toward where they think danger might be coming from. The ears pivot independently of each other, so one ear may be facing upwind while the other is facing downwind.

In terms of sight, a deer's vision is not so much better than ours, only different. For one thing, their eyes are located on either side of their head, not on the front of their face like ours. This allows them to see 310 degrees around them at all times. Deer can essentially see something that is directly behind them, when they are facing forward. The downside is that this makes it difficult for deer to focus on a single point.

The night vision of a deer is much better than ours. This is a huge benefit to them, when they feed during the early dawn and dusk hours.

Finally, deer see colors differently than we do. Biologists tell us that the deer's optical system sees mostly in yellow. They also can perceive the color blue, but they are unable to see the colors red or green.

Deer can see ultraviolet colors that humans can't, especially ultraviolet blue. Unfortunately, most new camouflage clothing is made with ultraviolet brighteners. So, while wearing camouflage will keep other hunters from seeing you, the ultraviolet brighteners cause you to glow in the eyes of the deer. They can see you even more clearly than if you weren't wearing camouflage.

Fortunately, you can purchase special detergents that will wash out the ultraviolet brighteners from your camouflage clothing, so it is more difficult for deer to see you. The detergent also helps mask your odor.

Dude, You Smell: How to Deer-Proof Your Body

Human beings just naturally smell bad. Anybody who has not taken a shower in a couple days knows this is true. We spend a fortune trying to cover up our odor with fragrant shampoos, soaps and deodorants. But, no matter how many times we wash, eventually our own stink will return.

While this fact can be a problem if you ride on the subway, it is even more of a problem when you are out in the woods trying to stalk deer. The sweet smelling products we use to make ourselves more presentable to other humans is like clanging a bell for deer, alerting them of our presence.

Staying downwind from deer is one way to keep them from smelling you, but any experienced hunter will tell you that the wind plays far less of a role than you might think. When it comes to their own survival, deer are pretty smart. If they are in an area in which they sense danger – and remember they have excellent hearing and vision – they will circle around the area to make sure there is nothing upwind from them that could harm them.

In addition to the commercial products that we wear, deer can also smell the gasoline on our hands and clothes, the cigarette smoke in our hair and on our clothes, cooking odors and a million other smells that we either can't smell or don't pay attention to.

While deer may have the sensory advantage in the woods, man has the benefit of superior intelligence in the laboratory. Years of hunting have given the hunter valuable insights on how to use the deer's sense of smell to bag him. It is a well known fact among the hunters that, aside from deer rattling, deer calls and decoys, using scents to attract, lure or mask your own scent from the deer's nose remains one of the most effective methods in bagging your dream buck.

There are many commercially available scents that you can wear to mask your smells. These scents mask your body's odors with aromas that are not threatening to deer – such as apple, pine, earth smells and other odors. There are also products that contain enzymes, which neutralize your smells, so deer don't smell anything.

The use of scents, including scent blocks and scent eliminators, cannot be over-emphasized. The deer's keen sense of smell, along with his nimble legs and sensitivity to the presence of stalkers, predators and hunters make him one of the most elusive targets a hunter can encounter.

Among these attributes is the power of his sense of smell, which is considered his greatest strength and biggest asset. Ironically, it can also be his weakest and most vulnerable point. In fact, most hunters go to extra lengths to use the deer's sense of smell against him, and to the advantage of the hunter. This is not an easy job, considering that deer have also mastered, to a certain a extent, the ability to distinguish lures and baits from the real thing.

Finally, while you can use chemical sprays and neutralizers to mask the odors on your body and clothes to improve your chances even more, it's important to consider the types of food you eat before heading out into the woods. If you are lactose intolerant, for example, you will want to avoid any dairy products that can cause you to become gassy. Similarly, a big bowl of chili on the night before your hunt is probably not a great idea, because it can cause you to pass gas. This type of odor can waft on the breezes for hundreds of yards and alarm deer to your presence.

During the off season, experiment with different foods that don't produce gas in your body. Everybody's digestive system is a little bit different, so what works for one person doesn't necessarily work for someone else. Then, once you identify food that is "safe," try to stick with those foods in the days leading up to your hunt. Not only will it help mask you from the deer's sensitive sense of smell, but it will make you more popular in the enclosed spaces of the hunting stand.

Using Deer Scent to Stack the Odds in Your Favor

We noted earlier that deer communicate with each other using sounds, such as bleats and grunts. But, they also send messages to each other through smells. Deer have glands that can emit strong-smelling aromas that send messages to other deer, such as a female ready to mate with a male.

This is good news for the hunter, because we can use these smells to stack the deck in our favor. Both artificial and natural scents can be purchased and used as bait, so that you can attract deer to your stand location. These scents mimic the odors that are emitted by the deer's glands, and can fool them by sending false messages. These scents can be purchased at most hunting supply stores or online. You can also sometimes get them from other hunters, which is why it is a good idea to develop relationships with other hunters throughout the year.

The most effective scent for luring a big buck is the urine of a doe in heat. It is particularly effective during the rut, when deer are in a state of sexual excitement.

One effective technique is to drag a rag soaked in the urine of a doe in heat behind you as you walk to your stand. You can effectively leave a trail for a buck to follow, which will lead him directly to you. This is one of the most effective ways to set yourself up for success.

When you get to your stand, hang the rag on the branch of a tree in a clearing. That way, when the buck arrives at your stand area, he will be more likely to come out in the open to see if he can find the doe in heat.

You can also dab the trunks of trees in the area near your stand with the urine of estrus does. This scent is from does in the ovulation stage. During the rut, bucks are on the lookout for these does, so they can have a successful mate.

By dabbing the trees in the clearing near your stand, you can attract bucks directly to you. Once they arrive, they are usually in a state of confusion, because they are desperately looking for the estrus doe, which isn't there. This sometimes causes them to be less cautious than usual, and gives you a better opportunity for a kill shot.

The type of scent you use also depends on the time of year. Earlier in the hunting season, for example, the urine of a doe in heat will not be effective, because the rut has not yet started. In this case, simple doe urine can be an effective scent, because it can attract the buck's curiosity.

Another technique is to create a mock scrape. Look for a tree limb hanging over a deer trail. Use a branch to scrape down to bare ground, then pour the deer scent onto the ground, as well as on the limb that is hanging over the trail. Bucks use these scrapes to mark their territory, so in many cases, they will be attracted to your mock scrape to see what other bucks in the area are up to.

Be careful anytime you handle deer scent, however, because a buck won't be fooled by it if you mix your own odor in with the doe scent.

Minimally Evasive: Top Ways to Ruin Your Hunt

Even experienced hunters sometimes fall into bad habits. That's why it's so important to keep an open mind when planning and conducting your hunt. Conditions on the ground are constantly changing, and the successful hunter is the one who can adapt to those changes quickly and effectively.

We tend to gravitate toward the areas where we feel the most comfortable or where we have had success in the past. This is natural, but it is important to resist this impulse, because the deer community is constantly changing, and as hunters we need to be able to read those changes and adapt.

One of the biggest mistakes you can make is focusing on only one scrape or rub. While bucks mark their territory with these signs, they don't always come back to them on a regular basis. Remember: A fresh scrape indicates that a buck has been in the area recently, but it doesn't necessarily mean it will be coming back anytime soon.

Another error is hunting in an area just because you saw bucks there in the past. During the rut, a buck will travel many miles in a single day in order to find a mate. Even during the rest of the season, the movements of bucks can be unpredictable, to say the least. The best way to find bucks during the rut is to find out where the does are. That's because sooner or later the bucks are going to show up there.

Does tend to congregate in areas where there is a lot of food. These "doe pockets" are great places to set up your stand, because eventually one of these does will come into estrus. When they do, a buck is sure to come calling.

Another mistake is trying to move through woods that are too thick. Deer have the advantage over hunters, because they live in the woods year round. They are used to moving through thickets and areas that are densely overgrown, whereas hunters only visit these places a couple of times per year.

Don't make the mistake of trying to go too far into the thickest part of the woods. Not only will it be difficult for you to move – and you will make a lot of noise while you do it – but, it will be next to impossible to get a shot off once you finally find a deer. A better idea is to stick to the edges of thickets and wait for your buck to appear.

Finally, most hunters get accustomed to only looking for bucks in the morning and evening hours, and will let their guard down or even go back to the lodge during the mid-afternoon hours. But, bucks don't have wristwatches. They can be looking for estrus does just as easily during the mid-day hours as during the morning and evening. Make the most of your hunting time by staying on the hunt all day long. Many hunters have bagged their biggest bucks during the "off hours".

Advanced Cloaking Techniques: How to Be Invisible

Paying attention to the way you smell is important. Using neutralizing scents is one way to prevent deer from sensing your presence. But, there are some other techniques you can use to improve your chances of not being spotted.

The first is to practice being still. You can buy all the expensive odor neutralizers you want, get the best camouflage in the world, and build your stand so deer will never see it, but the moment you shift around or snap some twigs under your feet, it is like shooting a cannon off to a deer.

Improve your chances by practicing being completely silent. Set aside some time every day or once or twice a week to sit quietly without making any sound. It's not something that comes naturally to most people, but it's a skill that needs to be developed.

Breathe silently, keep your eyes wide open and be hyper-aware of everything around you. Once you start to really listen, you will be amazed at the noises you take for granted when you aren't paying attention. This type of hyper conscious state is how deer are all the time.

Another way to make yourself invisible to deer is to put yourself in a situation where the deer are going to be so distracted that they won't pay attention to you. The rut is the most obvious example of this. When bucks are stalking does in heat, they have only one thing on their mind: a successful mating.

You also can position yourself near distracted deer by finding an area that has rich food sources, such as fields that have plenty of grains and seeds. Fields of corn, oats, wheat, rye and other crops are excellent places for deer to feed. Other well-liked feeding spots include fields of sunflowers, canola, and soybeans.

Using scent, decoys and deer calls are another way to draw the deer's attention away from you. Some states even allow hunters to leave bait to attract deer, although this is not legal in all areas. You should check your local hunting regulations, before using this technique.

Another great way to invisibly track deer is to use deer cameras. These are motion-activated cameras that you leave in the field. This type of camera takes pictures of deer when they move through the field of view. You can either return to the field to retrieve the camera later, or some more advanced models will transmit images directly to your home computer, so you can keep 24-hour surveillance on the deer in your hunting areas.

Many deer cameras will time and date stamp the photographs, and include information, such as temperature and whether the barometric pressure was rising or falling at the time the picture was taken.

You can use deer cameras that take still photos or cameras that shoot high definition video, depending on your budget and what your needs are. Deer cameras are a great way for hunters to scout deer while remaining almost invisible.

Here's a nice buck I got on my trail camera near Minong, Wisconsin

9 THE RUT

Ask any hunter and he or she will tell you the rut is the best time to hunt the biggest bucks. That's because this is the time of the year when the bucks are on the move, looking to mate with the does. Even the most mature and cautious bucks, who never venture out into the open at any other time of the year, will occasionally make an appearance in broad daylight during the rut.

The rut can be broken down into three phases:

The Pre-rut – Throughout the rest of the year, non-dominant males will travel in small groups, foraging for food and providing protection for each other by being ever vigilant for predators. But, during the pre-rut, these groups of bucks will begin to break apart. Their antlers will begin to harden, and they will scrape them on trees and branches. This is the time when bucks make scrapes to mark their territory, and use their scent to attract females.

During the pre-rut, which usually occurs between the last couple weeks of October and the first week of November, bucks will begin to get more aggressive with each other, as they battle to establish dominance. This is generally referred to as the "chase phase".

The Rut – This is the period when the does begin to go into heat. Not all does go into heat at the same time, but at any given time during the rut there are at least some does who are ready to breed. During the peak period of the rut, roughly 1/3 of all the does will be in heat.

The doe is in heat, also called estrus, only for about 24 to 36 hours. During that time, the doe is anxiously looking for a mate. If she does not find one, she will cycle down, and the process will begin again, in about 21 to 30 days.

Dominant bucks become much more careless during the rut, especially at the peak of the rut. Their hormones cause them to chase after receptive does regardless of where they are. They will cross roads, fields and walk right out into the open, if they think there is a doe to be mated nearby. In some cases, the normally cautious buck will walk right under your deer stand during the peak of the rut. There have been cases of bucks walking right past hunters, because they are so distracted by the mating process.

The Post-rut – As the rut winds down, the hormones in both the does and the bucks decrease, and their activity returns to normal. Bucks stop scraping and marking, and they once again become more cautious and go into hiding. Groups of non-dominant bucks re-form. Pregnant does prepare for the winter's gestation.

It's Go Time: Why Deer Biology is Your Ally

Deer season coincides with at least part of the rut, because that's when it's easiest to hunt deer. Bucks are at their least cautious, and are on the move looking for prospective mates.

Deer biology causes males to become less tolerant of each other and more aggressive during the pre-rut. They begin to battle each other for dominance and the right to breed with the best females. They literally will lock horns in order to defeat each other. This causes a distinctive clicking sound, which can attract other bucks, who want to see what is going on. This also tells dominant bucks that other bucks are nearby.

Hunters can attract deer during this phase by rattling antlers together. You can buy artificial deer antlers at your local sporting goods store, but natural antlers tend to work better. You may also want to try a "rattling bag". They can be easier to carry than a set of antlers, and are easy to use.

When you rattle the antlers together, the noise carries on the wind over long distances and captures the attention of all the deer in the area. Many will become curious, and will naturally gravitate toward the source of the rattling.

When you rattle your antlers, it's better to rattle them gently, instead of making a big racket. This causes the big bucks to think that the fighting is between immature bucks that can be easily dominated, so they are more likely to come out into the open.

Buck decoys are another effective hunting tool during the rut. It's hard to exaggerate how aggressive dominant bucks can become during the pre-rut, as they prepare for mating. Even the sight of another buck can cause them to become enraged, and they will often charge into an area in order to challenge them. Because they are much less cautious than normal, they will often mistake a decoy for a challenger.

The pre-rut is also the most effective time to use deer calls. Grunting challenges a dominant buck's authority, so it can cause him to seek out the buck who is calling him out.

A tending buck will make a different kind of grunt, as he is pursuing an estrus doe. This is the signal for the doe to stop, so she can be mounted. You can mimic the tending buck by making a series of short grunts.

Bleats are used by fawns and does, to let others in the area know about potential danger. You can also use bleats to mimic estrus does who are ready to mate.

During the rut, once a male has found a female, he will follow her around wherever she goes. This is called the "locked down" phase. During this period, the buck will abandon his normal routine, and shadow the doe as she feeds, drinks and seeks shelter, waiting for his opportunity to mate. This can last anywhere from a couple of hours to a few days.

Bagging the Trophy Buck: Why Patience Is Its Own Reward

All the work you have put into preparing and scouting for your hunt is about to pay off. It's finally time to bag your buck. The pre-rut and rut are the best times to find the biggest bucks, because they are out and about like no other time of the year. It's a pretty safe bet at this point that if you see a doe during this period, a buck will not be far behind.

During the fall, bucks leave their solitary wanderings, and return to the community of does and fawns. They will stay on the outskirts of the areas where does congregate for a period of about two weeks, waiting for the telltale glandular smells that indicate the doe is ready to become impregnated.

It's been said that during the rut, to find the buck all you need to do is to find the does. But, not every doe will have a buck trailing her. As you observe the does, if one is casually walking along without showing a lot of interest in the trail behind her, there probably isn't a buck trailing her. You should focus your attention on another doe.

But, if the doe is spending a lot of time looking back up the trail where she came or off to the side, and her ears are perked in that direction, it generally means there is another deer in the vicinity. It could simply be her fawns or other does, but odds are it could be a buck. Now is the time when your practice in sitting quietly pays off.

It can take up to an hour or more for a buck to finally make his appearance. Despite his excitement, the buck will still want to make absolutely sure there are no predators in the area, before presenting himself out in the open. At this point, it's your job to simply sit quietly and not give away your position. If you have done everything right up until now – masked your smell, built a stand that's out of the deer's line of sight, and prepared yourself for long periods of quiet sitting – all of that hard work is about to pay off.

At a certain point, your buck will appear. He may be tentative at first, or he may charge into the area filled with lust. It depends on the buck. When he does, slowly move your rifle into position, bring the buck into your crosshairs, and wait for your shot.

A moving buck is much more difficult to hit than a stationary buck. If possible, wait for him to stop moving, so you can make sure you hit your mark. Don't wait too long, however, or he could get spooked and run away. At just the right moment, gently squeeze your trigger.

If you've put the time in at the shooting range, you should be able to hit your mark with a single shot. If you miss the deer altogether, you probably won't have time to get a second clean shot off. However, if you have a second chance, you should take it. But, you don't want to just "throw lead" into the brush after a retreating buck in the hope that you might hit him. This is not only potentially unsafe, but if you injure the buck, you may not kill him. This will cause the animal to suffer needlessly.

Whitetail Deer Social Structure and Its Benefits

The uninitiated can walk through the woods for days, and never see a single deer or even any evidence that a deer has been in the area. But, for the experienced hunter who knows what to look for, signs of deer can be so plentiful it is almost as if there were billboards posted every 25 yards screaming, "Look here!"

One of the easiest signs to find is scraping on trees and shrubs. Bucks will make scrapes to mark their territory, to declare their dominance over other bucks in the area, and to attract females. They will chew on the low-hanging branches, and then lick the branches to scent them. Bucks will also leave their scent on the scrapes. They will return periodically to their scrapes to look for signs and scent of other deer.

Whitetail deer begin to leave a chain of scrapes about three weeks prior to the mating period. The first of the scrapes are usually made impulsively by the bucks in response to finding doe scent, evidence of another buck, or other stimuli. About two weeks before the mating season begins, the buck will begin to make primary scrapes, which are larger and carefully cleaned of vegetation down to the raw soil. These are the scrapes that bucks will revisit often to clean them of debris, mark them with fresh scent, and check for signs of visitors.

For the hunter, looking for fresh tracks around active primary scrapes is a great way to locate dominant bucks. It usually means the buck has been returning to the scrape, and it could be a good location to scout out a place for your stand.

Another sign to look for are rubs. Bucks will rub their antlers up against trees or bushes to strengthen them, and to remove the velvety outer coating that forms on them. Look for fresh velvet at the bases of trees and shrubs, which show signs of having been rubbed, as well as for fresh tracks. These indicate that a buck may have recently been in the area and could still be nearby.

Finally, when tracking a doe that is being pursued by a buck, the first buck is not necessarily the only tending buck for that doe. There could be others, so it could be worthwhile to wait for a second or even third prospective suitor to appear. And, while the first buck to appear may be the dominant buck, in some cases bigger and more mature bucks could be among the others following her. It all depends on the situation.

In deer social structure, bucks are continuously battling for dominance. But, that doesn't mean only one buck is the king of the hill and earns the right to breed with all the females. All bucks are looking to breed, and there may even be opportunities for the lesser bucks to mount does, given the right circumstances. For the hunter, this means that it is worthwhile to continue to scan the area, even after one or more bucks have appeared. Your trophy buck could be further down the line.

10 BUCK FEVER

The first time you spot a big buck while you are hunting in the woods can be a life changing moment. Your heart might start beating faster, your palms might get sweaty, or you might even start to shake. This is a common affliction among hunters known as "buck fever". Whether you successfully bag it or not, you will always remember the thrill you feel when the majestic creature steps out into the open.

Bucks come in all levels of maturity and different sizes. Some are young bucks with small antlers, and are just learning how to survive in the woods. These will be easier to hunt, but they are not as desirable as older, more mature bucks with grand racks who are experienced in the ways of the wild. It takes real skill – and more than a little luck – to bag one of these beauties. But, if you do, you will receive the admiration and respect of your fellow hunters.

Antlers are a secondary sexual characteristic that are used by other deer to identify the animal as either male or female. Only bucks have large sets of antlers. Generally, the older and more mature the buck, the larger the antler set, although heredity and nutrition also factor into antler growth.

The desirability of a rack increases with the number of points, inside spread, mass and symmetry. An outdoorsman association called Boone and Crockett developed a standardized measuring system to "score" these traits. The higher the score, the more desirable the rack is.

When you talk to buck hunters, it can sometimes seem like they are speaking a language all their own. For the uninitiated, it is easy to become lost when hunters talk about the rut, the rub and the scrape. Once you start hunting more, you will soon find yourself using those terms more often.

One term you will sometimes hear is when a buck is called a "shooter". This simply refers to the fact that the buck is mature enough and has a good enough antler set to be worthy of harvest. Antlers are measured by the number of "points" they have. These are the antler projections that extend at least one inch from the edge of a main beam or another tine. The more points a buck has, the more valuable it is. You may have heard people refer to a "10-point buck". This means that it has 10 points on its antler set.

10 point buck.

Another term you may hear occasionally is “cull buck”. This refers to a buck that is genetically inferior to other deer on private lands that are managed for quality or trophy deer. On many private hunting lands, any mature deer that has fewer than 10 points is considered a cull buck, and is not worth hunting. But, it is still worth your while to track cull bucks, because they can sometimes lead you to trophy bucks.

Finally, deer have a series of glands that excrete scents used to communicate with other deer. These glands are located in the forehead, between the hooves, and on the inner part of the deer's hind leg.

Deer use these odors to recognize other individual deer in the group. These odors can tell the other deer the individual's sex, social status and reproductive condition.

Where to Find Your Trophy Buck

Trophy bucks, or those bucks that are most sought after by hunters, get to live to be old and dominant, because they are skillful at eluding and evading hunters and other predators.

One of the most effective ways to bag your prize trophy buck is by searching for buck trails. Be on the lookout for points leading to a ridge or a hill that juts down into the plains. Better yet, look for a trail that leads to water frequented by deer to quench their thirst during summer.

Deer trails under power lines are a giveaway of deer who feed there. You may find a trail parallel to the line, and about five to ten yards back into the woods, where bucks wait until dark to venture out. Bucks usually pass through bunches of small trees. When you spot a tree stripped clean of bark, chances are a buck has passed through in that direction. Scout around for unobtrusive signs of a buck trail like tracks, bent grass, or messed up leaves. Then, follow that trail in search for another rub.

Check the terrain thoroughly, and make mental calculations on where the buck was headed. During early season there may be presence of a tunnel corridors coming from thick, elevated and rugged land. Bucks usually bed here, near open feeding areas. Mark each rub on your map, until you can anticipate the buck's movements. Scout around for ambush spots on route, like a path that is channeled into a narrow area.

Often big bushes with tree branches overhead yield areas with a buck's scrapes. Ability to detect fresh scrapes will make your hunting easier.

Thorough knowledge of the trail is also a big help in bagging your buck. You have to mark the spot where deer signs are: the scrapes, the rubs, etc.

The base of a tree usually is the place where rubs are found, while the scraping of deer hooves create scrapes in the form of patches on the ground. Scrapes found in bushes, means that the deer has already staked his claim on the area as his turf. Licking branches are generally found above scrapes.

Always look for the freshest scrapes, when buck hunting. Check on abandoned logging areas, natural clearings in forests, creeks, knolls, and fields. Staging areas on level, but sloping ground that is dry, minus the rocks and thick grass could also be a possibility. Search for a series of scrapes made through a route. The best place to put your stand is where a line of scrapes is found.

Your trophy buck

The first step to getting your trophy buck is defining what a trophy buck means to you. If you are just starting out hunting, it could mean any mature buck with a rack of more than 10 points. For a more experienced hunter, a trophy buck could mean one with 140 B&C points, which is much more rare, and could take a lifetime of hunting to find. Another goal may be to get a record-setting buck, so that your name will go in the record books.

Many hunters opt to cheat the system by participating in a "guaranteed" hunt. This is when you hunt with a highly skilled guide on hunting grounds in which bucks have been cultivated, and hunters are assured of getting at least one kill during their hunt. If you are an inexperienced hunter, this expensive option may be the way to go for you.

For those hunters who have respect for the sporting aspect of hunting, buying a buck is not the right thing to do. Instead, tracking and bagging a buck on your own terms has more value. If you can afford to hunt on private land, you are probably going to see more bucks, because they have been inaccessible to other hunters. If your budget only allows you to hunt on public land, look for places that are far from roads, and are difficult for other hunters to reach, because of the terrain, swamps, rivers or thick vegetation. This is where you will find your buck.

Obviously, the more scouting you do during the off season, especially right before the pre-rut, the better off you are going to be, once the hunting season begins. Setting up deer cameras is a great way to get started, but there is nothing better than actually spending time in the woods looking for marks, scrapes, trails, beds and other indications that bucks have been in the area recently.

Another important tool you will need is a good set of binoculars. Combined with a high-quality scope, powerful binoculars will let you identify and field score bucks from much farther, compared to using your eyes only. Having a good set of binoculars greatly increases your range.

Another way to improve your chances of getting a great buck is to spend as much time in possible in the woods during hunting season. A lot of hunters will schedule their annual vacation time, so it coincides with hunting season. That's because the more hours you are on the hunt, the better your chances are of getting your buck. Most hunters will tell you they would hunt every day of the season if they could, and a lot of hunters do!

The last recommendation for finding your trophy buck is to be patient. As you become more skilled in hunting, you will find yourself in the presence of many magnificent bucks. But, if you indiscriminately kill the first bucks you see, or you "settle" for bucks that don't meet your own trophy standards, you are going to fill your tags with smaller bucks, which you will ultimately find unsatisfying.

Patience is the hunter's greatest tool. Training yourself to wait for the right buck at the right moment is what will separate you from the pack of ordinary hunters. To help you keep in control, focus on the type of buck you are looking for, and what you are going to do with it once you find it. Imagine the kill shot. Visualize the antlers hanging on the wall of your den or garage. Think about how your freezer will be filled with venison for the entire winter. Make it worth your while to wait for the right buck.

Early, Mid and Late Season Deer Hunting: Advantages and Disadvantages

The period just before and during the rut is the busiest time for hunting season. It's when deer are most active. It is also when there are more hunters competing for the same bucks. Opening day of the hunting season is also likely to have a lot of people in the woods.

Many experienced hunters prefer the less crowded periods that occur between opening weekend and the pre-rut, and from the post-rut to the end of the season. That's because there are far fewer hunters in the woods, and you have a better selection of bucks all to yourself. Depending on where you are hunting, weekdays tend to be far less crowded than weekends, and Tuesdays and Wednesdays tend to be the least crowded of all, for some reason.

The weather will be nicer during the first part of the season. But, many hunters prefer tracking deer in cooler weather. This is because many times deer will congregate together in deer yards when the weather gets really cold, in order to conserve energy and take advantage of the best feeding areas. This can sometimes make it easier to find big bucks.

The other advantage of hunting in winter is snow. Deer tracks are easier to see in the snow, so the hunter can more easily follow deer trails as they lead from their beds to their water supplies and back. The snow also tends to muffle sound, so deer will be less likely to hear hunters from far away.

Some hunters don't like to venture out in the winter, because of the cold. But, the fact of the matter is that there is no such thing as bad weather, just inappropriate dress. When you dress for severe cold – with many layers of air-trapping wools and other insulators – you can keep yourself warm even in the coldest of temperatures. In some ways, the best times to hunt are the times that most hunters consider to be the worst.

Hunting for bucks in the winter is in some ways easier than it is during warmer periods. This is because after the rut is over, bucks return to their normal patterns of behavior, and become more predictable. Their primary focus in winter is to find food. At the same time, the food supply is dwindling. So, to find bucks in the winter, all the hunter really needs to do is find a rich food supply, set up a stand or blind, and wait. Eventually, a buck will come out of its bedding area to feed, and when it does, you will have your shot.

During the winter months, deer will also seek out spots where there is a lot of sunshine, so they can warm themselves and conserve their energy. So, on sunny winter days, you will want to look for clearings that are close to food supplies, preferably in an area where there is a field next to a dense forest. If you can find these conditions, there's a pretty good chance you will see a buck on a cold, sunny winter's day.

Keep your eyes on the weather reports during winter, as well. As we have stated, deer can anticipate changes in barometric pressure. As a winter storm approaches, they will often feed in a frenzy, as if anticipating being snowed in for a couple of days. If you can get into the woods in the 6 to 18 hours before a winter storm hits, you can improve your chances of bagging a trophy buck.

Still hunting is also a proven technique in winter, because with the fresh snow cover and the leaves off the trees, it is easier to see deer in the forest. Of course, it makes it easier for the deer to see you, as well. But, with a good set of high-powered binoculars or a good scope, you can see them from farther away than they can see you, and you may be able to get the drop on them.

Kill Shot: Bagging and Tracking Your Buck

Once you have your buck in your sights, you should aim for the area just behind the front shoulder blade, about a third of the way down. The quickest way to kill a buck is to shoot it through the heart and lungs. It is a pretty good target, and you have a much better chance of killing your buck, if you shoot it here.

Where to place your shot.

You can kill your buck instantly, if you shoot it directly through the spine or windpipe, but this takes a lot of skill. If you neck shoot your deer without severing the spine or damaging the windpipe, there's a good chance he will survive and run off into the woods, never to be seen again.

Headshots are another way to kill a deer, but they have two disadvantages. The first is that the target is a lot smaller, so it's easier to miss. If you shoot at a buck and miss, generally it's bye-bye buck. The second disadvantage is that you can damage its rack, and if you are planning on displaying that rack as a trophy, you have just ruined your chances of doing that.

In most cases your best bet is going to be a shot into the buck's chest. In most cases, the animal will survive the initial shot, but will drop after running about 100 yards or so, due to internal bleeding, or possibly damage to the heart, lungs or other critical internal organs.

When you shoot your deer, try to see where your shot hit the animal. Usually there will be a blood splatter that identifies the location. If you shot it in the back leg or hind quarters, the animal probably will survive. But, if you made a good shot into the chest, it usually will jump into the woods, and then run for a little while before collapsing.

Resist the impulse to run into the woods after it right away. If you made a good shot, the animal will die quickly. But, if you made a bad shot, an injured deer could run much further away than if you just let it lay down and bleed. This could make it more difficult, or impossible to find the deer. Better to just wait in your stand a bit, and let nature take its course.

The easiest way to track the buck you shot is by following its blood trail. This will usually lead you to the spot where it has collapsed. Another way is to look for breaks in the brush, or just listen for kicking or grunting. If the animal is still alive when you arrive, wait a few minutes before approaching it. In some case, the animal will jump up and run away or even charge the hunter. Neither of these are desirable options.

If, after a few minutes, the animal is still lying on the ground and is breathing, you can finish the job by firing your rifle into its heart. When the animal's breathing has stopped for several minutes, it has died, and you can begin field dressing it.

11 DEER HUNTING GUIDE MASTER CLASS: ADVANCED WHITETAIL TACTICS

Up to this point, you have gotten enough information to plan, scout and execute a successful hunting trip. In this section, I would like to give some final tips, so you can move from being a novice hunter to one of the elite whitetail deer hunters in your area.

If you want to find the biggest bucks, you have to teach yourself to think like a buck. When you are doing your scouting, think about what you are looking at from the buck's perspective. Where is the food supply? Where is the nearest watering area? What would be the best places to bed down? How can I tell if there are other bucks in the area or have been lately? When you become the buck, you gain a perspective that most hunters never achieve. And, it will help you understand buck behavior so you can track and find the biggest bucks in your area.

Finding a strategic deer stand placement to hunt from can be rewarding, once you have found the right spot. You will need adequate knowledge of the deer's movement pattern, his strengths and weaknesses, as well as his feeding and bedding habits. You should also be familiar with the buck's travel habits, the areas he prefers to traverse while on the trail, and things that he is wary of.

Plan your hunt for stands. Give careful thought to the entrance, as well exit areas when choosing a deer stand. The less obtrusive you are, the less chance you'll spook your buck in the process.

You should always remember the various food sources available within the area. Hang several stands that you can utilize in anticipation of change of food sources. When farmers start harvesting their crops, or acorns begin to drop, the deer will begin utilizing other food sources. They could also abandon their current bedding areas, and move to a different location.

The direction of the wind plays an important role in deer stand placement. Watch the wind carefully. A crosswind is favorable for hunting, if it blows perpendicular to feeding and bedding areas.

For evening stands, you'll want to hunt on a trail to, or overlooking a food source. Most of the deer are bedded during daytime. They begin feeding just before dusk, to avoid being seen. The majority of these mature bucks are reluctant to feed during daytime, to avoid undue exposure.

To avoid detection while walking out to your stand, use natural features in reaching your stand. They can be in the form of creeks, ravines and standing crops. Use them to the fullest, and as quietly and stealthily as possible.

The next thing you have to pay attention to is the use of camouflage clothing to blend with the environment and avoid detection. Wear detergent free clothes. And, use human scent eliminator to reduce your scent as much as possible, as the deer are equipped with a sharp sense of smell. Any scent emanating from a human will surely drive them away.

Walk through the woods naturally, but carefully. Deer are wary of human voices and metallic sounds. Natural sounds, like the breaking of a twig, are probably okay. They are used to them. But, too much creaking and stomping could arouse their suspicion. The less unnatural noise you make, the better off you are.

Be alert, and be watchful. Use all of your senses when tracking down a potential trophy buck.

When you are rattling your antlers, do it softly, not loudly. An experienced buck is going to know when somebody is trying to fool them into thinking there are fighting males nearby by loudly clacking their antlers. Instead, rub the antlers together gently. Then softly move them back and forth against each other. This more realistically recreates the sound of two young bucks rubbing their antlers together, and is more likely to have a big buck come running to see what's happening.

When you find scrapes and rubs, take caution not to contaminate them with your own scent. If a buck returns to his scrape and smells your odor there, because you touched it or got too close, it probably won't return to that scrape again.

Speaking of scrapes, they are some of the best places to find bucks just before and during the rut. That's because scrapes and rubs are some of the primary ways bucks alert other bucks and prospective does that they are in the area. And, they almost always return to their scrapes, just after it rains. That's because the rain will wash away much of their scent, and they will want to replenish it to establish their territory and attract females.

Growing and maintaining proper food plots for deer can be a nutritional asset to the management of deer densities. If you are hunting the same area year after year, seed your prime locations by planting turnips, clover and other plants that deer love to eat.

Depending on the terrain of the area intended for the food plots, it seems to work better to plant smaller food plots that are about a ½ acre in size. The plots can be bigger, if the deer pressure gets larger. Planting plots along the woodland edges and inside the woods is recommended. It is also recommended to plant plots 200 yards or so away from heavy coverage. This will ensure that the big bucks and other deer that have been under cover will come out during rutting season.

Always be on your toes, and ready to change location. It is not always advisable to hunt on the same area year in and year out, without changing location. Just because deer were in a certain location last year, doesn't necessarily mean they will be there with the exact same patterns this year. Be ready to move. As the source of nourishment changes, so do the deer. Their movement patterns depend heavily on the availability of food sources, as well as other factors.

The deer movement patterns cannot be 100% predictable. His habits, his moods and other characteristics may be altered, depending upon situations and circumstances. The environment plays a vital role in the deer's make-up.

He thrives by instinct and senses. In many cases, he can outwit the hunter, because he knows the terrain better, is fleet footed and nimble, and can weave in and out of tunnels, ridges and thick foliage, which can never be done by humans. It will always be a battle of wit and speed, between the hunter and the hunted.

The hunting season will put a human's skills to the test once more, as the hunter arms himself with all the hunting gear and paraphernalia at his disposal. The thrill of the chase makes him sharper and more confident. Out there in the woods, the deer wait. And, between them the challenge is clear to the hunter. It is a game that man and buck play up to the very end.

Finally, the most important thing to remember about deer hunting is that it is supposed to be fun. It is a great way to get away from your busy world and reconnect with nature. It can be one of the most refreshing things you can do. And for most hunters, it continues to get more pleasurable the more you learn about it and the more experience you gain.

Good hunting.

ABOUT THE AUTHOR

Andrew Saari has been hunting deer in Northwestern Wisconsin for over three decades. He has a website that is full of deer hunting articles, tips, deer pictures and videos.

Check out the latest at
www.whitetailtactics.net

And, grab copies of the other books in this series:
How to Hunt Deer: Whitetail Tactics
Bow Hunting: Whitetail Tactics

ACKNOWLEDGMENTS

Cover photo © Tony Campbell - Fotolia.com

10 point buck photo provided by deepspacedave/Pond5.com

Where to place your shot illustration provided by lantapix/ Pond5.com

Made in United States
Orlando, FL
12 December 2023

40735158R00085